UNITY LIBRARY 8 ARCHIVES
C0-AOA-864

The Living Sea Scrolls

An SOS Book

The Living Sea Scrolls

Spiritual Strategies for Living

"An inspirational voyage into the sea of spirituality"

SALLY O. SHARP

Trust Publishing

UNITY SCHOOL LIBRARY
UNITY VILLAGE, MISSOURI 64065

10/94

Copyright ©1993 by Sally O. Sharp.

All rights reserved. No part of this book may be used or reproduced in any manner whatsoever without written permission except in the case of brief quotations embodied in critical articles and reviews. For information address Trust Publishing, P.O. Box 24568, Minneapolis, MN 55424-0568. 612-929-5484.

Printed in the United States of America.

Library of Congress Catalog Card Number: 92-062378

ISBN 0-9634910-0-8

First Edition: March 1993

Bookstore

BL
624
.S53
1993
c.1

To Jeff Bolin, my husband and best friend, and to my "bringers of hope:" Samuel, Tabear, and Celia

God is my protector,

God is my light.

God is with me

Every day and night.

As I go within,

Eternal love begins.

God and I are one,

And it never ends.

—Sally O. Sharp

Table of Contents

Acknowledgments

I wish to thank and express my gratitude to all those who have helped me see my book to completion. To my husband, Jeffrey Thomas Bolin, and step-children, Matthew and Jessica Bolin, for their unconditional love, guidance, and support; Jan Nygren Kohls for her enthusiasm and encouragement; my mastermind partners, Laurie Eittreim, Barbara Laporte, and Gail Merritt, for their affirmations and shared vision; my sister, Rebecca Sharp, for her understanding and friendship; and especially to my editor, Bob Homer, for his insight, talent, and dedication.

To all who have helped in writing this book and to all who have helped me on my spiritual path, seen and unseen, I give my thanks.

Preface

SOS! SOS!— Help is needed! I am drifting from land, my foundation of life! I'm in the midst of turbulent waters, searching for a way to come home! My attempts are diminished by fear and desperation!

At one time or another, we all have been lost at sea. We struggle to the best of our abilities to find land. Learning to blend the sea with the land is learning to blend our spirituality with living. We all are spiritual beings. At times we become lost and drift from our center. Now, no matter how far we have drifted, it is time to discover ***The Living Sea Scrolls***— the great universal truths, and live the strategies that will bring love, hope, and happiness into our lives.

We are given many opportunities to expand our level of consciousness. Often there is so much preoccupation with other activities that we forget or never really know why we exist. What is our purpose? Confusion, insanity, and fear abound. It doesn't have to be that way. By turning inside we find answers. Wisdom is gained. We see the light.

Within each of us, there are places of untapped knowledge and ability. We have to be ready and willing to take steps in a new direction. In both happy and sad times we touch, we feel, and we learn. By opening our hearts and minds we discover the creative and loving potential we possess.

We grow up differently, influenced by certain beliefs, customs, and traditions and, yet, there is a common truth; the same common truth found in many religions. Ultimately, we have the same goal: to become at one with God. We just arrive there in different ways and at different times.

The Living Sea Scrolls is about believing and becoming. This book is designed to help those who are seeking direction and serenity in their lives. The scrolls came to me as I gradually pursued my spiritual voyage, trusting in the light to guide the way.

I have walked in many shoes and my shoes no longer fit. I have found that my footprints in the sand reveal my truest identity. Now, I need to share with you ***The Living Sea Scrolls***, that have helped me reach the shores of harmony and peace.

Together, we can change the meaning of SOS as a desperate cry for help to mean the Sea of Spirituality— a place of love and serenity.

—Sally O. Sharp

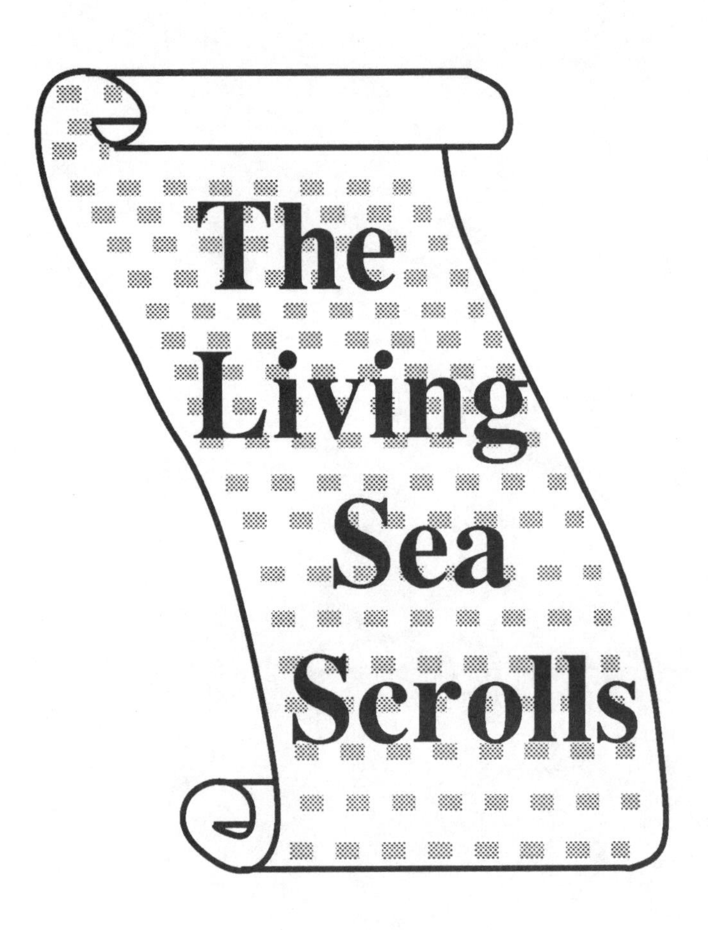
The
Living
Sea
Scrolls

Welcome to the journey. We will work together. Our purpose is to live the truth, to open up our hearts, to look at the wisdom within, to find and trust God: to become one, to become the spiritual beings we were meant to be.

So many people ask so many questions. **The Living Sea Scrolls** *will answer them; fulfilling the longing to know, to search and find the truth. As simple as it sounds, the truth lies inside your soul— your soul that is connected to God.*

The Living Sea Scrolls *bring wisdom, love, and truth. I look forward to our relationship to bring goodness to our world, our world that needs comforting and direction. It is up to every individual to make his or her choice— to choose the path that leads to oneness with God.*

Let God be the power for all. Ask for God's protection and direction. We are only messengers. You will make a difference in people's lives, helping them to be alive. At times it will be easier than at other times. At times it will be challenging. At times it will be rewarding. You are strong and gifted! I send my love and energy!

—A Bringer of Hope

The Living Sea Scrolls

Alone

eeling and being alone is going against our nature to be at one with God. When it is happening it is very real, confusing, and sad. Many souls try to escape from the feeling of isolation. To feel you do not belong under any circumstance is very overwhelming. We are really never alone. We have to look inside and muster up enough love and courage to know that we deserve to be one with our Creator.

The way we treat our fellow kind aids in our feeling of belonging. Going against one another is not our purpose. When actions and good deeds are done to aid others, we are then working with the universe. As we move rapidly in our lives, we forget these principles. This adds to the lonely feeling.

Do not make people feel more alone than they already are. Touch others to assure them that you care. *The more you give to others, the more you will receive.* Feel the presence of God. Call upon the energy of the universe and you will be supplied with the strength and love to carry you through. Trust and watch the emptiness be replaced with companionship.

Attraction

Everything around you is a reflection: a reflection of the object itself. If you have love and goodness in your heart, you reflect love and goodness. If you have respect and humility for yourself, you reflect respect and humility. Each thought you have carries an energy that is sent out to the universe.

Remember, thoughts held in mind, are reflected outside of yourself. Keep your thoughts positive and guided with love, honesty, and goodwill towards all of humankind. Bring what you want in your life first to your thoughts, and they will manifest themselves. Your actions reflect your thoughts. Let all thoughts vibrate with love. You can have true happiness and serenity when you let go of the idea that material possessions can bring happiness. Know that happiness comes from within and not from outside ourselves. By creating good for others, you create good for yourself.

Like attracts like. The positive energy you reflect attracts the positive energy of others. You will find that your positive thoughts instill positive thoughts in others. You will find unity among yourselves. When all thoughts are centered around God, then you have found your one true attraction.

Belief

e look in the mirror and for years we are not sure whom we see. We question the reflection. As we work through our lessons and work our way to finding explanations, we learn we are at one with God. We can have an abundance of riches, inside and out, if we allow our highest good to come into our lives.

How is it done? *The first step for any growth, anywhere and anytime, is belief in yourself.* When you love yourself you are loving God's creation. We were meant to be at one with God. We were meant to share in love and happiness. Open up your heart and let the universal energy of love pour in.

Blessings

lessings are bestowed on all, but many people do not know of these gifts. They are blinded. Blessings can come in many different packages. Because they are so different, often they do not look like blessings. The wise soul will know its blessings. Those who are trapped by their own limitations and thoughts do not see the beauty and the truth of these wondrous gifts.

We create our own environment from which good will shower us. The wise soul makes the best out of every situation. We often look at others and feel they are more blessed than we. Let the truth be known that we are all blessed with an abundance of gifts. But we all are blessed with different gifts; gifts God knows are the best for each of us. Create the world you want to live in from your special blessings and you will have it.

Blessings begin with every breath and step we take. Living and sharing in the creation of the body, mind, and spirit shows gratitude for the blessing of life itself. Show gratitude for the many gifts we receive. Give thanks and feel the realization of the blessings which come to you. See from a different angle. Put on new lenses with a new perspective. Open your eyes as you open your mind. Trust in the power of goodness; the power of God.

Work with what you have and pray for the blessings you need to be brought to you. Every path has its own course. Learn to tend your course and make a difference in your own life. This will bring in love and peace. You will then make a difference in the lives of others. When we start looking at our blessings and not comparing them to the blessings of others, we find that more blessings come to us. Walk, listen, and be truly blessed.

Blossom

he seed has been planted in you. Now let it grow and blossom into that beautiful flower that you are. It takes both rain and sun to provide the nutrients you need. Feel the presence of God surround and engulf you. With each bloom there is new awareness. Rise above the challenges and blossom. Put your mind toward reaching for the stars. As you set your goals and standards, ask God to lead you on your path for your highest good. *Whatever color and type of flower you are, you are important, for there is only one of you.* The earth needs your unique qualities and specialties. Bless others with your soul and your gifts. The seed you were born of was a seed from God. Let all your blossoms bloom into their full magnificence.

Boundaries

oundaries are needed in all areas of life. They provide a way to protect and nurture the soul. We are given the gift of self-love. This is not selfish love. That is different. This is God's love telling us to respect and honor ourselves.

When you use boundaries honestly, you are taking care of yourself. And once you learn to respect and honor your own boundaries, you can respect and honor the boundaries of others. In truth, this is saying that you love yourself and that you love others. Every soul has its own boundaries. *Respect your own boundaries and those of others.*

Change

o cleanse your thoughts and make changes, you must be willing to look at what is under the surface. To reveal yourself and accept your true form can be very painful. It is through pain and honesty that you reach a new level. A level where self-acceptance is embraced. Once the cleansing of old beliefs is begun, a new path will follow. Once the awareness is made, you will advance in wisdom.

Walk openly to new beginnings. Change is inevitable. Many resist change for fear of the uncertain. Change makes the process of life unfold. By accepting new growth, we leave behind what is not working. Sometimes we are forced to change without any control over the situation. It could be through a painful event. Our eyes may be blinded because of the pain. Through these times the soul can complete a phase of learning and attain wisdom. Sometimes, it is hard to understand this process on a physical level, but the soul knows what it needs for its development.

The same is true when wonderful events happen. The soul can move to higher vibrations in joyful as well as painful situations. It all depends on how the thoughts and actions are used throughout the process. There is a lesson in every situation. You have the choice to decide whether or not you want to grow from it.

We tend to blame others or God for our problems and tragedies. The undeveloped soul does not realize that these occurrences happen for a reason, usually from our karma and way of thinking. *Some say they can't see God, and yet God is in each of us; visible to all who put fear to rest and faith to work.* It is important to build positive and loving thoughts in our mind instead of creating fear within ourselves. Be a positive influence on others.

The beauty of growth is the beauty of renewal. As we begin to change, we begin to experience new feelings and vibrations. Hopefully, change is taken in the steps of wisdom. When we move forward on our spiritual path, we begin to grow. The beauty in change is in how one looks at a situation. Making changes can be very difficult. As the soul learns to trust in God, faith will prevail.

Faith is something that can be observed, but it must come from within. It is an inner peace inside that words and feelings cannot truly describe. Those who have put faith in their lives know the true definition. *Fear is dispelled when faith resides in the heart and soul.* As the soul learns to trust, it will know the power of faith. It is troublesome when the soul loses sight of faith. To not practice faith only brings confusion and restlessness. It inhibits the change necessary for growth to occur.

May all who are experiencing change bring their faith to the surface. For God provides all that is needed. Believe, trust, and see.

Choice

or some it is difficult to look in the mirror and see themselves. Until acceptance comes from within, the soul remains stagnant in development. When love and understanding are given to the soul, a new process takes place. The world seems different. The mind opens up to new avenues. Progress is made when the mind leaves one level and goes on to the next. Spiritual guidance is always available for those wanting and waiting to take the journey. The guidance is soft and loving, not harsh or threatening. Many do not understand this. Beliefs and opinions can be so strong that we put up a wall to shield us from any truth or wisdom with which we disagree.

Each being has the choice in what direction to take. Sometimes we learn by taking the wrong direction. The important part is that we learn *by doing*. What is the best way to recognize the right path? By listening to the voice inside, the voice that speaks when respect is given. *If we do not treat our own thoughts as valid information, we discredit ourselves.* This is not the way to inner strength and love. *The beauty of life is having the choice to change what is not working and try something that does work.*

Commitment

ommitment to an idea, purpose, person, or thing brings results. To achieve inner joy we must commit ourselves to do what we need to do to meet our goals. With the help, love, and support from the universe, we can make progress. Effort and strength lead the way to growth and rewards. In times of confusion and hardship, we can choose to let go of the struggle and listen to the guidance of our inner voice. As we let go of our fear and ego, we learn to commit to our true goals. The soul that works with and not against oneself is the soul that will rise above the challenges.

But our goals must be realistic. Frivolous, ridiculous, or impossible goals are a waste of energy. We do ourselves a disservice by being committed to goals of this nature. The truth and wisdom of our inner voice will tell us which goals are worthy and which are but castles in the air.

Facing the true self takes an honest and open approach. Laying blame on others for our lack of commitment only prolongs the process of obtaining our goals. *We create our own happiness or unhappiness.* The beauty of life is that we control our own growth. Take time to look and see what new seeds of ideas have been planted within you. Let them grow and blossom. As the truth of new ideas come forth, review your commitments to your goals. Be willing to abandon old goals for better ones as your knowledge and wisdom grow. *Flexibility* is as important a part of commitment as is *steadfastness*.

Creativity

reate what you want by believing in yourself, and in the universe to provide what you need. Let go of any past fears or blocks you may have. Today is a new day to reach within and bring out the good. Take charge and change what is not working in your life. With progress you will find yourself surrounded by thoughts of peace and harmony, and soon you will be enveloped in a peaceful and harmonious environment.

Creating is the finest form of expression. Be an expression of God. Let your energy manifest into a creation that you can call your own. Expression comes in many ways, some seen and some unseen. In times of discontent and in times of tranquillity you can be productive by releasing thoughts into tangible items. *When the mind works with the soul, then the body creates.*

Blocks of suppressed energy are freed when the soul is allowed to express. When the expression is mixed with love, then a creation of beauty exists.

Children often are the true sense of creativity. Their world is full of unconditional expression. When we incorporate passion and creativity into our work and lives, we live a very rewarding life. We allow our inner selves to express outwardly. Our creativity is always changing and expanding as the soul expands and grows to new levels. When love accompanies the journey of expression, creativity is at its best. Go and create. *Be*.

Desires

our heart knows good from evil. Place your desires in the energy of light. Release any desires that are not for your highest good or for the highest good of others. Search within to find the desires of spiritual growth. Bring the beauty of balance into your every thought. As you fill your soul with divine wisdom and knowledge, your every desire of spiritual love will hold true. Take the steps to find that inner truth of knowing.

The desires of today will be the reality of tomorrow. *Free yourself from limitations and embrace the ideas that help you create your desires.* Walk with confidence and speak with love. Let God guide you to the path where your desires flow naturally. Trust in your journey as you take the steps to bring passion, talent, and rewards into your life.

Exercise

hen we were in school, we did exercises to "exercise" our minds. This, too, is an exercise. As you go through the day, be conscious of your every thought and every spoken word. Replace any negative thoughts or words with positive and supportive ones. If you cannot come up with any, then let them go. Release the negative energy both in mind and action. You will find your day will be more uplifting and inviting. God will be seen, heard, and felt. As you practice this exercise, it will become a way of living. Treasures will be apparent when the cleansing is done.

Practice the exercise of peace. Close your eyes and rest your mind. Picture yourself surrounded by a calming energy. Let the energy soak into your pores, filling your body with love and healing. As it goes throughout your body, experience the tingling sensations. Be ready to heal any negative emotion or sickness. This is a process. The more you love and take care of yourself, the more you can enjoy the abundance of living life to its fullest.

Practice the exercise of laughter. Laugh today. Wear a smile and let it start from the inside out. Have a new approach. Take time off from being so serious. Realize that we must enjoy the moment. Projecting too far into the future or concentrating too much on our troubles prevents the child in us from coming out. *Laughter is a stress reducer.* We all need more love, smiles, and laughter in our lives. Start with yourself. You'll find it's contagious!

Faith

aith is the belief in the power of God. *Faith dispels fear.* Go within and reach for faith. Your every need is provided. Shift to a new awareness. Discover the power within to lead you to safety. Turn to the light for answers. Let the light shine in the dark corners of fear. Take time to quiet the mind and allow the answers to come. *To have faith is to have God in your heart, peace in your soul, and strength in your body.* As you practice having faith, inspirations turn into ideas that bring solutions and gifts. Trust in your inner self. Your soul knows faith. Find faith and you will live the truth as a child of God; at one with God.

Fear

ear is a lack of belief in the power of God. *Fear has no power against faith.* Take time to calm the mind. Put hope in your heart and displace fear. You create your own fear by listening to outer circumstances. Turn to God for the comfort and security you need. Bring love to your body and mind by concentrating on your oneness with God. Step outside the situation and turn it over. Let God have control. Carrying around fear, anger, and resentment brings stress and sickness, emotional and physical. Let harmony flow through your body as you attract the light of hope and peace. God gives hope and you create the peace. With peace in your heart, your soul is at home. *Make a home built around God and there you will find the love you so desire and need.*

Forgiving

o love is to forgive. The ability to forgive is a true test of growth. When the heart and mind are in conflict, the body carries the stress of the situation. Carrying anger and resentment is not in the body's best interest. The body gets sick. If the resentment is carried for long periods of time, the body becomes a home for disease. Measures taken to prevent such action are recommended.

How do you learn to forgive, especially if much harm and hurt have taken place? Trust the universe to provide the proper action. Everyone will have their own actions. The wise soul knows that we reap what we sow. *When we learn to forgive others, we also learn to forgive ourselves.*

True forgiving comes from the heart. Words cannot create the feeling. Serenity replaces resentment and anger. The process of letting go differs for each soul. Some souls must experience different phases of hurt and anger for their own growth. Start looking at life with a new perspective. Let go of what you cannot control and accept your responsibilities. Peace and a shift in consciousness will come. This lays a smoother foundation for the next lesson on forgiving.

Some people work through their problems and disappointments better than others. They do not let the situation control them. They have strength and calmness. They work from a high level of consciousness. They have discipline in their thoughts as well as their actions. They have faith that God will work with them. The soul who moves toward forgiving and not toward resenting will come to a place of tranquillity and serenity. *Resentments, more than anything else, stunt spiritual growth.*

No matter how much you might think you know what is good for someone, it is not your job to force it upon that person. You cannot make someone forgive you or come to your understanding. The best way to do this is by the example that comes from how you live your life. If you truly forgive, then it reflects in your life and provides encouragement for those around you. During the times when you need to be forgiven or need to forgive someone, reach out and ask God to help you.

Friends

t has been said that a friend is someone who knows everything about you and still loves you. The love of a true friend is unconditional. The corollary is also true. You are not someone's true friend unless you love them unconditionally.

God puts true friends in our lives. It is our true friends that support us and give us strength when the going is most difficult. True friends are priceless gifts from God.

But choose your friends with care. Someone who may appear to be a true friend may not be. Check with your heart to see if the love and concern they show for you is real, or if there are other motives for being your friend. Be a supportive friend and set your standards high. Your friends are a reflection of you. When you share the company of others and there is good, then good will come from them. When you share the company of those that bring harm to others, then you are harming yourself.

Trust your heart to not only know if a person is a true friend, but also if you are being a true friend to another. God will help you. Open your mind to let love come into your life and you will have it. You deserve to be with others who share in your goodness. *When you practice unconditional love and forgiveness, you will attract others who express the same.* Be a true friend and find a true friend.

Frustration

his, too, shall pass. Change is constant. Know that you do not have to stay in one place. When you suffer from frustration, try to look at the root of the problem. Step outside the situation and see what is the cause. Be patient and kind to yourself. Do not try to force a solution. Answers will eventually come. Let the frustration pass and clear the mind before making decisions— unless the frustration is due to the indecisiveness. Many times we haven't received all the information that is needed to make a decision. Ask that God provide the resources to move you out of the challenging moment. *Take what you learn from every experience and use it to help you in the next situation.* God wants us to grow, and this is one way we do it. Move forward, not backward. Learn from your mistakes and continue having successes. We have advances and setbacks to teach and prepare us. Tomorrow is a new day. Greet it with gratitude from what you've learned today.

Gifts

ppreciating the energy that brings fulfillment to our lives is to appreciate every waking breath. With every breath and every step, we have the power to rise and develop our wisdom within; the wisdom that leads to the spiritual connection with God, the Almighty.

Witnessing a union of energy reveals the great mysteries of life. Witnessing the union of thoughts reveals the likeness we share and the unlimited potential we have. Looking within and reaching within connects the soul to the Infinite Spirit who created us.

Raising the level of vibration and consciousness brings a release of positive rewards to all who share in the radiant energy. Praying and putting a loving touch on the many hearts that need healing reaps a stream of positive flow. To give a gift is to receive a wave of God's desire. *A loving gift that is unconditionally given to another will be returned to you tenfold.* Take time and look at all the loving gifts that can be given and go spread the love. Not only will it spread and grow, but the true meaning of our existence will be answered. The rewards you receive will astound you!

The heart is at peace when the gifts given at birth as blessings from God are fully used. Every soul has many talents and unique skills that can be expanded. Experience the joy when you use these gifts to create an expression of yourself. Do not let fear get in the way. Have faith in yourself, and God will help you along. Be open to the divine wisdom that is yours. Bring forth your passion and your love and let the energy of creativity manifest into a creation of your own. Handle your ideas with patience, hope, and trust.

Know when the time is right the success will become apparent. With persistence and positive attitude, greatness comes. Trust your inner thoughts and go with them. Your body is most in harmony when you follow your heart. Carry with you strength and be guided as you go to create good. Call upon your unique gifts to let your ideas manifest. Know that you have the power within you to bring dreams to reality through your gifts. You are a creative spirit. You can bring solutions to your problems. Go beyond the limits. Visualize your hopes and goals. Surround yourself with the light of love; the light for direction. When you receive an idea and it feels right in your heart, then follow your hunch. *Ideas are of no good until they are put to use.*

Guidance

esults happen when the belief in everlasting life is truly accepted. Everyday challenges can be met with more understanding and ease. The struggles may still be difficult, but understanding takes place on a soul level. The lessons to be learned are goals to be achieved. Your soul was put here to work out the lessons and live a happy and fulfilling life.

The walk through life needs to bring in higher vibrations to continually ease the conflicts. How is this done? Through opening new channels, new avenues, and new solutions, you will be guided. Also, souls are constantly guiding other souls by providing assistance and direction.

More and more people will be looking for spiritual guidance; guidance that is soft and unthreatening; guidance, that will enable all to be accepted on their own paths. The foundation of this guidance will need to come from God, our source. Healing is essential. We can carry emotional scars or blockages from our past. *The more we are released from the past, the better the physical body will function.*

Happiness

appiness is the result of blending love with faith. God is love. When we live our lives with the belief that all are equal in the eyes of God, we can love others as we love ourselves. *Love starts within and grows outward.* To see beauty in all and to walk the path of wisdom brings the soul to true awakening. As we share the moments of harmony, energy surrounds us in complete serenity. To respect all creation is love. May we find more love in our hearts.

Happiness is finding yourself and knowing the truth. The truth that you are at one with God and will always be at one with God. There is no reason to live in fear and distress. Walk with God in your heart and you will be protected. Happiness will fill every cell in your body. Even in turbulent times a soul can have true happiness. There is a place of serenity. It resides in your soul. It is knowing that divine order is taking place. It is having a trust in the universe. Find your happiness by living your spiritual path today.

Healing

e are surrounded by the light of healing. Healing comes as one breathes in and, slowly, exhales the divine energy of abundance. The riches of life are stored in each of us to enjoy.

The body and soul can be healed by sitting in the silence of one's thoughts. Reach within and bring to the surface the inner gifts that are available. Open our hearts up and let the energy charge every fiber. Feel the beauty of our presence. Feel the beauty of God. Clear the mind long enough to appreciate the wisdom of the soul. We all need to give and receive more love. *There is never too much love.*

A smile represents more than just a smile. A smile says, "Love exists in my heart and I want to share it with you." We forget to see our blessings if we run through life too quickly. This only prolongs the process of reaching inner harmony.

The soul has many riches. All needs are met in abundance if we walk the path where the spirit of good exists. Blessed are those who are on this path and help others find the way. The way to wear a smile is in truth and sincerity. It is a comfort to know we are truly protected and loved by the Infinite Spirit. Walk safely through the journey by opening the heart to receive all the abundant gifts.

Healing begins with you. Listen to what you say to yourself. Do you *speak* with love and kindness? Watch how you treat yourself. Do you *act* with love and kindness? With discipline, we learn to nourish our bodies and minds with healthy food and healthy thoughts. When you are ready to begin the healing, center all thoughts toward love and balance. God is love. Know as you heal, emotions are released from the body. If there is anger, resentment, guilt, or shame to be released, let it go. To be centered, continually turn your thoughts back to love . All healing is spiritual. It is to make us whole again; change darkness to light. Angels are channels of light. Let their light come to you and bring rays of healing.

Hope

oin hands across the world. Join hearts across the world. Put aside differences. Appreciate that we are all beings of love wanting love and needing love. Look at each other with love and hope, not with hate and despair. Do not judge, just be. Wrap positive thoughts around each other for comfort and warmth. Come out of the cold and dark to the sunlight of hope. Grow with vibrations of peace and spread them to everyone. Be a transmitter of love and hope will occupy your heart.

Independence

elebrate the independent spirit within you. At the center of your being is the connection to the universe. When we learn we are independent, we come to know we are all truly one. Love exists in all. God exists in all. *Those who have not turned inward to find themselves are lost, but never abandoned.* Know that as you turn to the light you discover your free spirit. *By practicing self-love and meeting your own needs, you automatically give love to others and help them meet their needs.* As independent souls, we come together in spirit.

Journey

lessed are we that share in the abundance of love that God provides. If people could see beyond their own troubles and look further, they would see a place that exists in harmony. Souls need each other to give and receive love.

How does one measure one's attempt to reach for that space where only loving and peaceful thoughts reside? The measure is up to the soul to decide. Inside of us there is a very deep place. You will not need to ask if you have reached it when you are there. You will know it. It is an opportunity that every soul, young and old, has the ability to reach.

You must have harmony within yourself before you can project it out to others. One must know one's soul and pursue the path of unity with God by living, actually living, life. *Even the most troubled souls long to know the answers to life. They long to know they are truly loved. They long to know that there is a better way.* Everyone can have a beautiful journey.

Kindness

e kind today. Everybody could use a dose of kindness. Express your thoughts with love and let your actions be soft in nature. A simple good deed will refresh the spirit. Send a positive thought to your neighbor. Find peace at home and let it spread to all with whom you come in contact. Kindness goes farther than hatred. Care about the words you speak and the energy you release. Learn to express yourself in a different way. Make sure your expression is based on love, even if you are frustrated. Communicate as an adult who wants peace and resolution. Inspire the hearts and souls of others to follow your lead. Resist the temptation to behave in a selfish or mean way. Let kindness come naturally.

Knowledge

earching outside oneself will not bring answers. Go within and discover your soul of intelligence. The school of education exists inside. Find a way, with God's help, to receive the information that is stored at the core of your soul. Be in a balanced state and ask for the doors to be opened. Have a clear mind and a pure heart and let the knowledge be expressed. Your potential will surface as desire and discipline increase. *With an open mind free of judgment and fear, answers and ideas appear.* Ask for the protection and guidance of our Creator and a path of goodness will follow. Accept the love of the universe. Give love to the universe by attending the school of your soul. You must go within before the knowledge can be shared outwardly.

Learning and Growing

here is a time for learning and growing. If you walk the path with God in your heart, truth and beauty will unfold before you. Trust, and the way will be shown. Keep the mind and body clear and your mission will prevail. The art of giving and seeking will bring results. Rest, relax, and then move. Move in the direction where serenity can come and the heart can be at peace. This comes from doing the work that brings you physical and spiritual satisfaction. Steps that you take to seek wisdom will provide the foundation.

Clear the inner self from all fears and worries. Ask God to show you the way. Messengers are here to assist. Information and direction will come. Take the steps needed, reflect, and move accordingly. With each step taken, the love of God surrounds you.

Learning and growing will come naturally. When you cease to expand your learning, you are not using your potential. The mind then becomes idle and more difficult to change. To grow means to open up and feel new energy. One trace of new energy can be a beginning for new creations.

Inspiration comes from many directions. *Deep inside of us there is a wealth of information and unique ideas. The key is to tap into this potential.* Why let it go to waste? Let the ideas bring helpful and loving assistance to yourself and others. The more we help others, the more help is given back to us. When we go against this principle we are in conflict with our soul.

Lessons

o experience life means to experience ups and downs. The key is to make the downs as few as possible, with the least amount of disturbance. *The more balanced we become, the more we have consistent happiness and hope.*

The trying times may last an hour, day, week, month, or even longer. You have the choice to decide how long. You have your path and your lessons to learn. Some lessons are more difficult than others.

Some souls have developed more wisdom and can see more clearly.

Have faith: God is there for you. Seek his wisdom and follow his will for you. You will find you can then cope with the trying times. The lessons learned from these times will make you grow.

Limits

imits are the product of a closed mind. *There are no limits.* Set yourself free in your thinking. Say you can and you will. Your efforts will pay off. Believe and become. *Change your thought and your behavior will change.* Find a role model and be a role model for others. Open your mind and test your capabilities. Do not settle for anything less than what you want. Harmony is yours if you want it. Be willing to let go and give up what is not working so you can let new opportunities present themselves. Strength comes from open-mindedness. Broaden your horizons and see that there are no limits, except the ones you make.

Listening

When you listen to your soul, you are in balance with yourself. This attainment shows wisdom. Listening within is the best guide available. When we listen to ourselves, we are making contact with God. It takes insight to distinguish listening to our *wants* from listening to our *needs* for growth and peace.

Our soul knows before coming into our physical body what is needed for our development. It is our mind that clouds and distorts the process. More and more souls will be working toward a kinder and softer way. Old ways will collapse and there will be new awakenings. Levels that once seemed unreachable will be reached. You can rise and make room for higher learning. Ultimately, blockages will make you stronger and consequences will help you reach new insights.

Listen carefully to what you are saying. Pay attention to what you need and what you are receiving to live a healthy and spiritual life. Our inner voice guides us, but we must listen. When we deny ourselves inner peace and joy, our lives become unmanageable and fearful. Learn to go within and connect with God. *Inside each of us there is a place of hope and strength. It is time to no longer look for someone else to bring us our happiness.* We have the potential to tap into our inner well of knowledge anytime we like. God gives us free choice with our decisions. Use the gift wisely.

Living

e walk the road of life with many questions. Our thoughts become our reality. If we believe in the Lord, the Almighty, and trust in God's guidance and wisdom, then we walk the right path. We are provided with all. We must look and seek the way; the way our Father has prescribed for us.

The body and soul that does not believe, cannot truly live. *To live is to love and to love is to have God in our hearts.* The soul is the heart of our existence; the soul that stores all. Place hope, faith, and love in the heart and you are living; living in the present. Living is receiving knowledge. Know that we are provided with an abundance of riches. Tapping into the soul's riches is tapping into the core of the heart. Therein lies the key.

When we unlock the passageway, we find ourselves on a journey; a journey to oneness with God. *To breathe as if we were at one with God, is to breathe life.* Share your breath of life with others, and let the riches overflow.

By knowing ourselves, we know God exists within our hearts, our minds, our bodies, and our souls. Add depth and dimension to your life by opening up to the riches of the universe. One merely has to breathe in life. Beauty and harmony can come in the most simplistic of ways. The most complex situation can be broken down into simpler parts by turning to our Divine Spirit and listening to ourselves.

The soul that learns we have the answers available to us is the wise soul. Answers are given when our thoughts are transformed into ideas. When we live with loving and peaceful thoughts, we will create loving and peaceful actions. Remember that our God is one of good; the highest good. It is our choice to hold that good in our hearts. May you be surrounded with the light of love and the light of direction. *The only true light that exists is that of God.* Hold on to it and walk in the light. Live your life as a child of God.

Love

f all the spiritual attributes, love is the greatest. Each being needs the warmth and support of the universal spiritual energy. Every breath of love taken in opens the way to fulfillment and enlightenment. Every breath of love exhaled opens the way for others. Spiritual love then expands into a powerful energy. The more it grows, the stronger it becomes. This is true of the soul. The more wisdom the soul attains, the stronger it becomes.

Every step taken represents a part of the growth cycle. When a step is taken with the love of humankind, the step becomes at one with the universe. When goodness is at the foundation of every step and every breath taken, there is no challenge that cannot be accepted. *The heart and soul remain intact when centered on the love of one another and in the love of our Infinite Spirit.*

It is in the darkness of fear that steps are taken toward the destruction of another. To turn all darkness into a flowing stream of the light of love would bring an energy too beautiful to describe. May all existing love-light beings share their sparks with all matter. When sparks hit someone or something else, they ignite more sparks. It then becomes a magnificent cycle. For one soul to grow in enlightenment makes another soul look at its own path. This leads more souls to become beacons of the light of love.

Strength comes when wisdom is gained. Every path leads to a solution. It is an inspiration to help all to the path where inner peace resides. Love is a powerful word that needs to be heard and felt by many. Many have been on a hard-traveled road. There is hope for all beings. The beacons of the light of love bring hope to those who have no hope at all.

To see souls reach and feel their own inner strength and harmony is love in itself. Faith is a starting place. Gentleness will occur on all levels. A peaceful approach to achievement will be everlasting. Attainment to one's purpose will unfold with every step and every breath taken. Love yourself and you will love others.

Condition your body, mind, and soul to work as one. Take time to maintain a healthy attitude and let it be reflected by the thoughts and food you choose to put into your mind and body. Walk a path where the foundation allows you to grow and not descend. Allow others into your life who bring light to your soul and not darkness. Reach for the stars and touch the energy of love as you transcend to your destination.

Speak of love: the love that exists in all. We all have the energy in us. To share love is to share ourselves. Spread love through all your travels. Spread it joyfully and unconditionally. You will be provided with protection and warmth. As you grow, so does your love and understanding. As we deepen our comprehension of life, we deepen our love of ourselves. We find compassion in our hearts. Illuminate the world by sharing a spark of love out of your soul.

There is an endless supply. *God gives back many times what we give.*

Love is the foundation of life. God is love. You are love. We were born to love one another. To love another we must love ourselves. In order to grow we have to come back to love. You don't grow by hating yourself, your neighbor, or the world. Love starts within and grows outward. When we go against our natural rhythm of love, we are out of balance. The universe is constantly showing us how to go back to love. Listen and see your voyage with clarity. Find the love in your heart and share it.

The ability to love is within our reach. Trust that you will see love as the foundation of all. It is the breath of life. As we breathe with life, we act with love. Understand the truth of life by living the truth. Believe in your heart and soul that we are all made in the likeness of God. Love one another. Make peace with all whom you come in contact. Forgive the wrongs of others so your wrongs will be forgiven. Love is the gift we all share. The more love pours out of our soul, the more love pours in. Go spread love to yourself and others. The rewards are measureless.

Luck

ucky. We all know people who seem to be very lucky. When the analysis is over, these people usually have the admirable traits of hope, discipline, and hard work. The lost and confused often falsely accuse the hard worker of being lucky. They do not see all the actions that go behind the results. When someone does something well, it looks easy and effortless.

Gifts do come to many, but in most cases, these gifts have been earned. They do not have to be understood by all. They just are. As you progress to a higher spiritual level, laziness and apathy go away and are replaced with movement and action. Watch a talented musician play a fine instrument with ease and grace. Is it by luck he or she plays so well? Of course not! The musician may have been given the gift of music, but the talent to play so well came from hours of hard work, discipline, and dedication. *In most cases, we make our own luck.*

Miracles

he power of love creates miracles. You are a miracle. Let your soul share in the miracles of today. Experience the power of love by loving yourself and others. On your path you will touch the lives of others, giving others love, hope, and trust. *All miracles start with love and build with hope*. When it is for your highest good, a miracle will occur. Believe and be ready. Accept the energy of love and the light of good. Encourage all to be open to the love of God. Find the miracles in your life. They are all around you.

Mission

o find your mission is to find enlightenment. Many know their missions as they know their names; others struggle and never know their mission. When the mind is clear and the body is in balance, clarity comes. An inner voice is heard.

Some souls complete their missions without ever realizing it. Others know they are taking steps to achieve a goal. When the heart and the mind work as one, peace occurs and the mission is completed.

Many along the path get sidetracked and through their own free will ignore their true desires. Serenity comes when we stay on course with our missions. When others see the serenity we have by being steadfast to our missions, we bring hope to them.

Patience, faith, and work on our missions results in a dream come true. May you take hold of your mission.

Mystery

The mysteries of life do not have to be mysteries. Mysteries are mysteries because we do not understand them. Understanding comes as the soul searches and achieves wisdom. A spark of information or an affirmation often is all it takes to get one on one's spiritual path where truth about the mystery can be found. Mysteries are dealt with as we come upon them. *With faith and acceptance of God's help, mysteries can be resolved, leading to a greater understanding of the truth of life.* While it is painful and frustrating to see some souls take longer or struggle harder to resolve their own mysteries, it is an individual process that they must go through. We can give our love and support, and share our growth and knowledge, but they must seek the answer.

Passion

iscover your gifts and carry the strength of the universe within you. *When you follow God's will for you, you will find the highest level of peace and serenity you have ever experienced.* New and exciting vistas will open for you. Your gifts will expand to new dimensions. You will experience a new level of excitement. This will be your passion.

This passion will fill you with gratitude. Be thankful for your breath. Appreciate who you are and face life with an energy of love. The more you radiate with a desire for life, the more life will treat you with the love you want. Unlock the potential you have inside and take the risks to find who you are. God is with you all the way.

Take time to relax and go within. Quieting the mind allows new energy to come. Enjoy what you do. Make your work a hobby. Add excitement to your life by living your life with passion. Use all your abilities. When you are bored, you know you are not challenged enough. The mind need not be lazy. Keep it sharp and focused. Let God be your starting place and then move outward. You do not have to be understood by all. As a spiritual child you never walk alone. God is within you and outside you. When you know this, all things are possible. Let go of the fears that inhibit your creativity. Invest in yourself by treating yourself with nurturing thoughts of love and respect.

Use your passion to stretch your mind by asking questions. *Figure out how to leave something better than you found it.* Decide what you want and go after it. Do not be limited with or by material goods. Use your mind to overcome obstacles. Treat each obstacle as an opportunity to grow and develop the creative spirit. Success comes in many different ways, but not always on the first try. Usually, when we don't achieve success on the first try, we learn valuable lessons that enable us to achieve a success greater than we had planned. You must channel your energy in the direction you want to go. Believe in yourself, and others will follow. Use your passion to tap into the resources that are stored in your soul.

Appreciate what you have and love what you don't have. Do not compare yourself to others. Trust in your own path and in your own creativity. Use your gifts and you will be given more. When you use your talents wisely, the soul is in harmony. All gifts are meant to be shared. Be good to yourself and you will be good to others. Your passion will give you the strength.

Past

look at the past will help explain the direction of the future. Your soul receives certain understanding and growth throughout it's evolution. Once the knowledge is learned it becomes important how it is used. Why do some refuse to learn from past mistakes and actions? "Fear" is usually the answer. With more insight into the everlasting life, fear will disappear. More people will feel safe on their journeys. You become joyful from the teachings of God and no longer want to live in fear. Positive loving words must be spoken. Good energy needs to be released and shared. Compassion will provide a start for those who are suffering and in pain. God takes care of all. Unfortunately, minds sometimes comprehend only what is apparent, therefore cannot understand why things happen as they do. Many are afraid to ask for help or direction, but it is there if only they would ask.

For the lonely who feel abandoned by their families, loved ones, friends, or society, do not give up hope. You are loved. You have friends: call them guardian angels or spirit guides. They will love you, care for you, and protect you. Your thoughts are heard. Your energy is felt. God does not abandon. God is the source of all love. Believe. Love, peace, and serenity are achievable and reachable to everyone, no matter where you are in your life.

Peace

e are not here to be at war with one another. While you may not agree with others, there is no need to have hate in your heart. The more we are at one with God the more open-minded and tolerant we are of others. Love and harmony equal peace. Peace starts with you. Do you have peace within yourself? *The first place to make peace is within your soul. Then you will carry peace wherever you go.* Peace is the result of trusting in the Lord. When the mind and body are calm, vibrations of love and harmony touch the hearts of others. Go spread your peace and watch your life change.

Potential

racefully bloom into the rich creation that you are. Touch the inner strength that lies inside, around, and behind you: it is your potential. We have a source we can go to, talk to, and pray to when we need help. God is available at all times for our every need. We might use other resources for guidance and assistance, but God is the force behind all healing.

We are often blinded by the magnitude of our problems. Our lives become filled with despair. We loose track of our potential. When the mind, body, and soul work together as one and let love and wisdom come in, the root of all problems can surface and be dealt with on a higher level. We face our choices somewhere in time. There is always a way for help and development. *The meaning of our existence is to discover the spiritual being we all are, and become at one with God.* We learn through our lessons.

We have potential that lays dormant. Open yourselves to the new energy and vibrations that exist. Simply listen to the voice inside. Surround yourself with love and goodness. Let all that does not bring you happiness be removed. Picture yourself receiving the gifts of abundance. We have the potential to grow to new levels at all times. *Do not judge yourself by someone else's potential. Utilize your own.* Create the path that will let you be you in your highest self.

Praise

ou are a gift, beautiful from the inside out. You are here for a special reason. *Know you are loved and you are loving.* Realize you are okay just the way you are; right now. Open yourself to the light of God and shine as a star; a star of love. Be ready to experience praise in your life. When you express yourself as a child of God only good will result. You can help make a difference in other lives. Know this and seek the road where all creations are equal. You are wonderful and needed today and everyday. Accept praise with grace.

Prosperity

There are no limits except those you create. You can have an abundance of riches when you live by the rule of abundance and not of limitation. You deserve to be blessed with prosperity. True prosperity comes when you are doing what your heart truly desires. When you are using all your talents and gifts with God as the foundation, prosperity will come. *Money is not the source of prosperity. It is only a tool.* You have the right to let the wind of spirituality push you to higher levels of abundance. Don't be afraid to sail off on the course that is right for you. A course that brings fulfillment to the heart will bring prosperity to the soul.

Purpose

Changes in *your* plan can be taken more gracefully when you are aware of the *soul's* plan. Develop new ways to look at the total picture to determine its purpose. Your level of maturity grows and your actions reflect the handling of changes in plans. Steps taken in acceptance and peace far outweigh steps taken in resentment and fear. Those who realize the purpose of their souls' plan progress farther to higher levels. When emotions are released, cleansing occurs and wounds heal. The highly developed soul uses every situation as a learning experience and accepts it as part of the soul's cycle.

Be careful not to judge others. You do not have access to all their data or their plans' purposes. You can serve only as a helper and must attend to your own purpose. When you start to create a superiority over others then you will be forced to deal with your own karma. *The mature soul prays for those in need of guidance and direction, and does not do the judging.*

During periods of the soul's cycle, the soul is faced with different situations in which we may fulfill our earthly wants, but lose sight of the purpose of our soul's plan. These decisions and choices can affect our ongoing growth. Many times we have to go back and regroup. Wisdom takes time and is earned. The beauty of all souls is the reaching of higher levels of wisdom where peace lies. To feel this level of happiness and true harmony within the soul makes one want to continue on this journey. Once this is experienced, the soul desires more of this harmony. *Only by keeping the purpose of our souls' plans in all our thoughts and actions can we stay on the right path.*

Rising

re you rising above the challenges of life? Or, are you being crushed by their weight? Why not ask God to carry the burden? Or, are you too proud? If God is willing to give you knowledge, wisdom, and direction, why wouldn't God be willing to carry your burden for a while? Ask God and the right answers will come. Be patient. Walk with confidence and let God do what is right for you. You are close to the mountain top; hang on and feel the energy of God get you there. Visualize your goal. Feel what it would be like to overcome your obstacles and be where you want to be, emotionally, physically, financially, and spiritually. *With God's help, you have the power to move mountains through prayer and meditation.*

Sea

he mystical magic of the sea. The sea is continually delivering messages to help any voyage be a successful one. Listen carefully as the elements of the land meet the elements of the sea. When the heart and mind become one, we sail a blissful journey. As a vessel sets sail, the rules of the sea become apparent. *Rules of the sea (the great truths) have existed from the beginning of time. It is up to each vessel to practice the teachings and carry the message to help other vessels on their voyages.*

Water to the soul is love to the heart. Water your soul with the sea of spirituality. Cross each passage with hope. Let courage be your outlook.

The sea will forever flow as your soul swims in this world of oneness. To understand the great mysteries of life, one must live the great mysteries of life. Self-discovery comes through experiences. Continuous wars are no solution. The power of authority is not force. The time has come for the world to wake up. Wake up to the power inside every soul. Let that power be of love for one another. Crises will continue until love is in the heart of every soul: 'til all return to their homes.

Foster all thoughts in the realm of understanding. Ask for the promises of the land. Hear the voices of all; hear the voice of one. Do not turn your back on others. No, turn your ear to them. Listen with compassion. Find compassion in your heart. Live with love. Give of yourself. It is time to bring the sea to meet the land and bring spirituality home. Where is your true home? It is with God, our leader. May we all follow the path of righteousness. Search no longer.

Self-love

aking notice of our strengths helps build our self-love. Nurturing allows healing to take place on a spiritual level. We were not always conditioned to love ourselves. The time has come where all living creatures need to love themselves as well as each other. Every soul has something to love. Every soul needs to be loved.

In times of difficulty, chaotic energy can create a downward cycle. We find it hard to love ourselves. Souls must unite and bring love and understanding back into the picture and let go of hate and resentment. The weaknesses we share need to be addressed. Let go of the bad and replace it with good. Let go of chaos and replace it with order. We need to improve our self-love.

Changes and good can come from any situation. The importance of growing is to learn and love ourselves. The path to oneness with God comes naturally. Every soul is different. Every soul has its own lessons. Every soul has a path. We can teach our beliefs, but wisdom is earned. First, accept your lessons and it will be easier to accept others. *Before trying to work on another, try working on yourself.* You can't love another enough to help him or her if you don't love yourself. We can help another by sharing our own growth and insight. The beauty of living comes from the beauty of self-love.

Self-love comes when we realize the importance of our every thought and action. The more we choose not to listen to our inner voice, the voice of God, the less we love ourselves. The more out of control we are in actions or words, the less we love ourselves. While lessons are happening continually, the way we choose to handle them makes all the difference. Ask for help and turn things over. Pour out energy of goodness and goodness will come to you. Do not measure all by what you see. Your efforts will be rewarded with self-love.

Sickness

n times of sickness, a cleansing takes place. Let the body rid itself of the toxic poisons and make room for health and harmony in every cell. Call upon the angels to help you in your healing process. They are messengers of God who bring light rays of miracles. Ask for their help and believe in their healing touch, invisible to some, but known in heart by all. *Embrace the energy with the desire to be healed, and as your soul heals the emotional body, the physical body responds.* Never give up hope. Even if you need medical attention know that the power of your thoughts mixed with the power of God makes the healing process possible. Be still and open up to your own angels. They may appear as radiant balls of light or by just inspiring a peaceful idea. Or you may simply feel their presence. Wherever you go and wherever you are, angels of love and healing are surrounding you. Ask with sincerity and watch harmony surround you both in thought and body.

Silence

isten to the silence. Hear the sounds of peace. Clear the mind and become a channel for higher energies. Reach for the stillness that brings contact with God. By quieting the mind, divine energies flow through us. Accept the messages of wisdom that are brought forth. Embrace the warm energy. You are just where you need to be. It is by divine order. Raise your consciousness to higher thinking. Watch the fears fall away. Watch your perspective change. Learn what is important. Speak highly of others or don't speak at all. Know your thoughts produce energy somewhere. Let it be the energy of love. *The world is in need of silence. Silence and love carry the message.*

Sounds

he world is full of sounds: some good, some evil, but most are unimportant. Tune in to only what you need to hear. Train your ears to receive only the good sounds. But not all sounds come from outside oneself; just as many come from within. Be open to your inner voice and the voice of God. Chimes of peace come from wanting the best for yourself and for others. Keep your body, mind, and soul in tune and radiate with vibrations of peace. Listen to the sea and what do you hear? Words of hope; waves of strength. Draw upon the unseen force for protection. Leave behind the storms and drift into the current of love, hope, and trust. Take the good sounds that you hear and pass them along to those in need. *Sounds of love leave vibrations of hope.*

Speaking

he tongue can be sharp and out of control. Harsh words leave scars. Buttons are pushed and emotions are triggered. It is important to voice your feelings in a healthy way.

Some circumstances seem unfair and our reactions may be strong. Go within and find yourself. Then speak with self-love and love for your neighbor. *When we speak peacefully, without hate and fear, others are more prone to listen.* Words have great power and should be taken seriously.

Expressing yourself is important. Let the expression be one of truth. The truth needs to be heard. The word needs to be spoken with love from the heart and not with anger from the voice.

Story of Soul

n the journey of life you begin to question your actions and your purpose for existence at different times. This is a good sign. When you connect with the universe and learn to flow with the energy, great accomplishments are made. Success comes from within and cannot be measured by outward materialistic goods. This does not mean the successful spiritual person cannot share in nice material things. All thoughts and intentions should be balanced.

To be in tune with the inner voice and the voice of the universe is the true definition of listening. The universe brings us answers on a continual basis.

It is the human who refuses to pay attention. The soul stands back until an understanding comes through.

The less developed soul faces growth at the same speed but does not necessarily learn at the same speed. To constantly bring awareness into our daily lives would make a consciousness so strong that even the most challenging goals could be reached. But each of us learns at our own speed. Finding and sharing the truth ultimately soothes the struggling and confused soul.

We cannot walk the walk for another, but we can lead the way. When peace and happiness find a home within your soul, you will instinctively know the strength of God; therefore, know the strength of your own wisdom.

Every road taken, rocky or smooth, has wisdom to be learned. Answers and help come from many different resources. Love, peace, and harmony come from one source: our God. It is the bad choices you make that lead to fear and harm. When your soul is rich in wisdom, fear and the choices which are not of God's will are eliminated. When fear is present, it is important to recognize it as soon as possible and turn it over to God.

The universe will take it away and replace it with comfort and direction. The mind must be clear and balanced to receive the new ideas and help that come forth. It works if you practice. It is much easier to have help than to try to conquer life alone. To express a need for assistance is a trait of the strong and not the weak. If you isolate and do not let in the universe's energy, you will not have serenity. Each phase of life will call on different wisdom to lead the way. The first step is the step for guidance. May all walk toward the path where the steps are taken through the wisdom and guidance of the Almighty, our Father.

Suffering

here is often disagreement between your physical body's desires and your soul's desires. When there is pain and suffering, it is hard for your intellect to accept certain situations. You wonder how God could let this happen.

Why do evil things happen to innocent people? This is a question that is often asked. Many times there is no answer to this question that we can discern. But one fact is certain: it is not God who causes the suffering. We must be compassionate and try to help troubled souls. Goodness can be for everyone and not just for a chosen few. How does one take the first step? By asking for God's help and to be shown the way. *Ask God what you can do to relieve the suffering of another.* Many times all the suffering person needs is someone who cares. Results happen when the suffering soul becomes willing to be guided.

But, sometimes when bad things happen to us, we are the cause. You might think there is no way you would choose to be in such a situation, but you are seeing only what you want to see, blinded by what is really happening. You must search your innermost regions. With all the honesty and humility you can muster, you must see if your suffering is being caused by your own will out of control. If this is the case, you must ask God what God's will is for you, and abandon *your* will for *God's will.* This may cause you even more pain. But, your soul can handle more than your physical body thinks you can handle. Take heart; this pain is temporary and will pass. As you find the right path again, God's path, your suffering will end. *God does not forsake anyone.*

Sun

ou are the sun. You shine brightly and bring light to others. You will always exist. *You make the world a better and brighter place to be.* The mystery of your being is found at the core of your brightness. Inside is the light that makes the outside light up. Radiate and share your beams of energy with others. You have the power to give life to others. Appear in your natural state, a ball of light. Reach for the stars and you will find the sun— the sun that is you.

Thanks

oday is a time for thanks. Everyday is a time for thanks. When we can appreciate the simplest of gifts even in times of confusion and hardships, then we move forward. Thanksgiving gives us the opportunity to help others and help ourselves. Those who share this moment with others can together celebrate the love of God. Take time to send loving thoughts and prayers to those who have no one with whom to share and to those who are lost in their lives.

The home can be a very special place to show your warmth and love. Let it be surrounded with love, without expectations and impatience. Holidays can be filled with undue stress when one loses sight of the real meaning. Take time to open yourselves up and enjoy each other. *For those who feel they are alone, open yourselves up to the presence of God. God will touch you and care for you.*

A soul that appreciates the gifts of living, the true gifts, will reap rewards from the gratitude. Prayers are heard and answered. Prayers of thanks are highly important. They work with the soul for the highest good. As with anything, just acknowledging the opportunity to experience the moment is of value. Be aware and respectful of all gifts offered to us. The wise soul can look at all situations as a way for personal growth and advancement. Those who suffer must know that the grief will pass and be replaced with invaluable insight and softer emotions.

Go all the way and you will find what you need. You will find what is always there: an infinite love and energy. For God forsakes no one. Give thanks for today; give thanks for you. For without you, there would not be this moment now. As you know, there will always be you. Your soul will remain forever. Treat it right, by first thanking God for your unique being, beauty, and potential.

Thoughts

elcome thoughts that bring warmth and joy into your soul. Learn to let go of thoughts that are troubling and disturbing. Practice concentrating on love and peace. Move your vibrations to higher levels as you open the passageway to truth. Let your actions reflect the thoughts you hold in mind. Know that the thoughts held in mind, produce after their kind. You create what you want. Take the steps to bring positive influences into your life. Release fears. Security comes in trusting in the Lord. When you direct your thoughts to God, your every need and request is heard. Thoughts are energy and they must go somewhere. The more the universe can share in positive loving energy, the closer we come to individual and world-wide peace. You and your thoughts make a difference. Use them wisely. Discover the power within yourself to change your life. By changing your attitude you set the energy in a different motion. When the attitude is changed for the better, better gifts come. Keep the mind healthy, and the body and soul will be healthy.

Let new thoughts be a reflection of your personal growth. Discover the world within yourself and then you will let the world discover you. Every soul has a journey to take. A journey that will be decided by you. *To realize we make our own happiness or unhappiness is to realize the truth.* The soul that is old and wise will know the meaning of this statement, and realizes it will grow only if this statement is put into practice. We are given many opportunities to expand our level of consciousness. Often we do not seize them. You have to be ready. You have to be willing. Willing to take a step in a new direction. Serenity is found when fear is gone. Serenity comes when you take the opportunity to grow. The mind that thinks it knows all, knows nothing. Walk in the light of sunshine. You can be the sunshine that spreads light wherever you go. You can make a difference in your own life and in the lives of others. Fatigue is replaced with strength. Anger is replaced with calm. Hate is replaced with love. Selfishness is replaced with generosity. All bad is replaced with all good.

Good thinking changes the way we look at every situation, even the ones that are bad and/or difficult. We learn a new way of handling our behavior. Results will only inspire the importance of the consciousness of our thoughts. All thoughts go somewhere. Keep that in mind always and remember you are responsible for your life.

Acceptance starts with love, love for being who you are. Each day is a new opportunity to love yourself and to grow in your soul; at one with God, at one with all.

Time

e in the moment. Live in the present. Make every moment count. Try to release the past and not project too far into the future. Relinquish control and let God be your source for protection and direction. Pray for others and pray for yourself. Be calm even in the midst of turbulent times. We go through experiences to become stronger and wiser. Be patient with yourself and others. Look for the best in every situation. Look for the best in everyone you meet. With love and trust at the foundation of your heart, you will become more accepting of the present moment. Walk with your eyes forward. Greet time with opportunities. We came from God and must be with God. That time is now. *Do not wait to be with God some other time.* Know you are with God at all times. It is just a matter of knowing.

Time is a block to many. If you are living life in fast motion, you are not allowing for tenderness and love. It is good to be productive, but it is also good to slow down long enough to express love and kindness along the way.

More and more people will be seeking a lifestyle where time will be used to provide for inner needs as well as outer needs. They will want work for a life that is more rewarding and joyful. Time with family and nature will be important. Making this happen takes discipline, especially if this is new to you. *Live in the present.*

Touch

ouch a friend with love. *Go out of your way to say, "I love you." Whether you choose to say it silently or aloud, speak it with love in your heart*. Appreciate people in your life. Appreciate nature. Appreciate yourself. Everyone is special.

Learn to see the good. Learn to bring out the good in others. Touch the universe with care and concern. Your touch of warmth spreads and makes others touch with warmth and love. Ask for more warmth and be guided to places of gentle touching. Hug a friend. Hug a child. Hug a pet. Yes, even hug a tree! Radiate from within and bring the universal love-energy to others.

Truth

he wise accept the truth and speak the truth, though it might be hard to face. The truth wins and comes to the surface. *We cannot run from the truth*. When you learn to be honest and true, life can be faced with courage, strength, and good intentions. Then loving results are achieved. If you turn to lies and deceptions, your life becomes self-destructive.

Speak the truth and the truth shall be heard. Truth will always surface. The truth cannot be silent for too long. *The higher self can always turn to the universe for the truth. God will speak. It is up to us to listen.*

Create an environment with only the truth and the highest good, and you will have it. Then you will be surrounded with purer energy and higher vibrations. The vibrations are in synchronization with your natural harmony. When obstacles present themselves; hold strong, and the truth will let you rise above them.

Trust

hen bonds of trust are broken, the damage goes further than the eye can see. *Honesty builds friendship; lies build distance.* Fear and shame are the roots of dishonesty. When you truly love yourself, the truth will be shown. Until self-worth is established, the truth might be too painful to face. When you lie to cover up something it might work for that moment, but in reality it eventually comes to the surface. The results are more damaging than if you were honest from the beginning.

To face up to something is difficult because you must own the truth. You who live your life on principles of dishonesty are weak and frightened. If you have been lied to by someone you trusted, ask why you were attracted to that person. It is painful to lose trust in a loved one or friend.

Forgiveness must take place for the relationship to succeed. This is often easier to say than to do. The confusion sets in when the one who has had an honesty problem is trying to come clean, but is put under doubt and suspicion. To bring up past mistakes over and over will eventually do as much damage as the lying.

To be strong, anger must be dealt with and then released. This will allow for new beginnings. Both parties need to understand each other's point of view. One is trying to be honest and change old behavior, and the other person is trying to build trust again but is struggling with old hurts. When both parties are willing to move forward, then harmony can be reached.

Change is taken gracefully when your soul's purpose is shared. New ways to look at the total picture come. Steps taken in acceptance and peace far outweigh steps taken in fear and resentment.

Unfolding

he mind is extremely fascinating. It longs to know answers, yet it does not always know the direction to take to find them. Every soul is on a different level. Some are more advanced than others. Advancement comes through wisdom attained through previous experiences. All souls are unfolding on different levels and at different rates.

You choose your path before coming into your physical body. Your path is a way for the soul to develop wisdom and become a soul for higher learning. All souls have a place for advancement. Do not be discouraged no matter where you are. If you are on the right path and doing the right things, your soul is unfolding on schedule. Be patient.

The beauty of life is when all souls work together in helping to create a welcoming place where everyone is accepted. A highly developed spiritual soul can show others the way— the way where a new start can transform into a beautiful journey. A smile or hug makes the surroundings more peaceful. Humor is essential for growth. It is important not to take any situation too seriously. Laughter cleanses the body and brings in freshness.

Dreams of hope and love can turn into reality with the help of God. Souls are never alone, even in the deepest valleys of loneliness. There are others waiting to help souls to unfold when the help is wanted.

When we get weary and our shoulders get heavy, we can use the universe to help carry our burdens. God works in mysterious ways. Because many souls are turned off or confused about the word of God, they don't ask for help. The earth needs to be restored with spiritual energy that allows people to be enriched by the universe's energy. With time, a troubled soul will seek out its own relationship with God and begin its spiritual journey. The starting point begins with inner awareness. Watching the way the path unfolds is an experience of beauty and strength.

Voyage

ords of wisdom come when the heart and the mind are in balance. There is a dawn after the darkness. Storms of emotions and storms of changes add insight to the voyage of life. It is the way we greet and accompany our storm that determines the outcome. Messages come from the great winds and the roaring waves. As the sea calms down so does the mind.

Once you have obtained hope, happiness, and peace in your life, how do you hold on to it without drifting? When the mind is quiet and still, the light is visible from within. The powerful beams of light bring the insight that takes and keeps us on our spiritual voyage.

Why

inding the purpose of your life and relating the soul to the body and mind makes you have inner peace. Once you have clarity, it becomes a reality of life. Life is no longer a mystery. There are still challenges, but they can be looked at in a different way from a clearer perspective. Understand and know that everything we do is for the sole purpose of becoming at one with God. *We are all God's children and must turn to God.* To express opposite vibrations is going against God's will.

Wisdom

isdom comes through every waking experience. The key is to stand back and take a look at what works and feels loving and right. Our souls are much less troubled when we treat them properly. When we go against God's will, it only creates turmoil and fear.

Our soul develops and gathers wisdom. It recognizes and stays away from negative influences and wrong-doing. The soul can constantly reach new vibrations and higher levels of learning.

Some souls are here to help other souls find their paths, lending assistance in that direction. It brings much peace and comfort to know your help and touch might be all it takes to believe in the Almighty. God is available for all and at all times.

It is important not to judge others. We are not the authority. All these words sound so simple but, for many, they are too far away to reach. More and more people on earth will be reaching out. The more positive spiritual energy that is expressed, the more the vibrations will flow smoothly.

There are all kinds of souls with different missions and different levels of wisdom. As your soul develops, the more at peace it becomes while growing closer in the oneness with God. May all strive for this goal.

Change in thoughts will change action. Put the idea out there and let it be loving and positive. Then watch what unfolds. The power of prayer is so strong. The more people who know this, the better. So many souls search for answers in all places, when in reality the answer lies within each and every one.

God is here: ready to assist and protect. God does not abandon or forsake any of His children. *Prayer can bring solutions that seem unattainable.*

Prayer can bring solutions that seem unattainable. Prayer can move mountains.

Beauty and peace lie in an unseen force— a force so powerful that it is indescribable. Faith is needed in all lives. With the faith of God, miracles occur. How do you teach children and souls that all they have to do is believe? The easiest way is by example, by being the spiritual beings we were meant to be. Often answers come by watching and learning from someone else. That is why we all learn from everybody and everything.

It is wonderful for those who have God in their hearts to share their wisdom with others, in hopes that they, too, can reach fulfillment in their lives.

Truth remains constant

In the Sea of Spirituality,

Beneath the surface

Of ever-changing tides.

Messages in the currents

Ageless, ever-present,

Seek the seekers,

Shaping vessels of love.

Within the sea caves

Of spiritual wealth,

Dwell the Living Sea Scrolls—

Discover the Treasure.

—Jeff Bolin

As I stood on the shore

And faced the sea,

The warm wind whispered

A message to me:

Bring hope to those

Who are in need.

Hope is the sunlight

And you are the seed.

—Jeff Bolin

About the Author

Using her initials *SOS,* which is also the international cry for help, Sally has created SOS books and workshops in the area of spirituality. She lectures on the positive ways to find the happiness and serenity we all are meant to enjoy.

Growing up in a small Kentucky town provided Sally space to reflect and create. In high school, Sally received the award for having the most school spirit. She earned her Bachelor of Science degree in three years from the University of Mississippi, graduating at age 20. She spent ten years as a sales representative and trainer in the apparel industry, both in Dallas, Texas, and Minneapolis, Minnesota. She then became motivated to leave the field of sales and pursue a writing and speaking career. She has two step-children and lives in Edina, Minnesota, with her husband, Jeff Bolin.

Her persistence and wisdom have seen her through both joyous and challenging times, steering her to the completion of her goals. Her lifelong gift of bountiful energy combined with the gift of spiritual insight has inspired Sally's creativity. She uses all her talents to help bring out the gifts and talents of others by showing them how to tap the realm of infinite power that surrounds us all.

Her SOS lectures and workshops, include such titles as *Seeking Our Spotlight, Securing Our Serenity, Secrets of Simplicity, Signs of Strength, Steps on Self-love, Seeking Out Solutions, Story of Soul, Sharpening Our Skills, Secrets of Spirit,* and *Structuring Our Senses.*

SOS Books

Order Form

If you cannot find ***The Living Sea Scrolls*** in your favorite bookstore or library, you can order a copy by completing and sending us the following order blank.

Your Name ______________________________

Address ______________________________

City ______________ State ______ Zip __________

Telephone (include Area Code): ______________________

(In case we have questions about your order.)

Quantity	Item	Price	Total
_____	**The Living Sea Scrolls**	$9.95 ea	________
	MN residents add $.65 Sales Tax per book		________
	Shipping ($2.00 for 1 or 2 books; $3.00 for 3 or more)		________
		Total	________

Please send your order and payment to Trust Publishing, P.O. Box 24568, Minneapolis, MN, 55424-0568. If you have any questions, please call (612) 929-5484.

SOS Audio Tapes

Order Form

Trust Publishing is pleased to offer audio cassette tapes featuring the meditations of Sally O. Sharp and the piano artistry of Larry David. They blend in an amazingly balanced harmony of inspirational energy and artistic excellence.

Your Name ______________________________

Address ______________________________

City ____________________ State ______ Zip __________

Telephone (include Area Code): ____________________

(In case we have questions about your order.)

Quantity	Item	Price	Total
_____	**Angel Whispers**	$12.95 ea	________
_____	**Tides of Love**	$12.95 ea	________
	MN residents add $.84 Sales Tax per tape		________
	Shipping ($2.00 for 1 or 2 tapes; $3.00 for 3 or more)		________
		Total	________

Please send your order and payment to Trust Publishing, P.O. Box 24568, Minneapolis, MN, 55424-0568. If you have any questions, please call (612) 929-5484.

Comment Form

If you would like to be notified when more *SOS* books are available, or if you would like to be added to our mailing list, please use this form to let us know. Also, if you have a comment for Sally O. Sharp, author of ***The Living Sea Scrolls***, write it on this form.

Send this comment form to Trust Publishing, P.O. Box 24568, Minneapolis, MN, 55424-0568. If you have any questions, please call (612) 929-5484.